HORSES
PAST AND PRESENT

MARIANNE JOHNSTON

The Rosen Publishing Group's
PowerKids Press™
New York

Published in 2000 by The Rosen Publishing Group, Inc.
29 East 21st Street, New York, NY 10010

First Edition

Book Design: Michael de Guzman, Resa Listort, Danielle Primiceri

Photo Credits: p. 3 © Tom McHugh/Museum of Natural History and © Stephen Simpson/FPG International; p. 4 © Orion/International Stock; p. 6 © Keystone View Co./Photoworld, Division of FPG International; p. 8 © Field Museum/Photo Researchers; p. 10 © Photoworld, Division of FPG International; p. 12 © The Natural History Museum; p. 14 © Laurance B. Aiuppy/FPG International; p.16 © National Musem of Natural Art/Art Resource; p. 19 © S. Maimone/FPG International; p. 20 © Mark Newman/International Stock; p. 22 © 1997 Digital Stock Corporation.

Johnston, Marianne.
        Horses past and present/ by Marianne Johnston.
            p.   cm. — (Prehistoric animals and their modern-day relatives)
        Includes index.
        Summary: Discusses the prehistoric ancestors, evolution, and some modern breeds of horses.
        ISBN 0-8239-5207-X
        1. Horses, Fossil—Juvenile literature. 2. Horses—Juvenile literature. [1. Horses, Fossil. 2. Horses. 3. Prehistoric animals.] I. Title. II.
    Series: Johnston, Marianne. Prehistoric animals and their modern-day relatives.
    QE882.U6J64 1999
    569'665—dc21
    [B]   98-19932
                                                                                                          CIP
                                                                                                          AC

Manufactured in the United States of America

2290883

CONTENTS

HORSES

Today horses play an important part in the lives of people all over the world. We ride them. We race them. We use them for work on farms. We even keep them as pets.

How long have horses been around? They've actually been on Earth longer than humans. The first horse **species** lived on Earth around 55 million years ago. Over time, horses have grown and changed. But they have been our friends and workmates for thousands of years.

Horses, like these, have lived on Earth for millions of years.

EVOLUTION AND FOSSILS

To find out more about **prehistoric** horses, scientists study **fossils**. Fossils are the hardened remains of long-dead animals. The fossils of ancient horses tell us a lot about what the horses of the past were like and how they are related to modern-day horses.

Horses have gone through many changes throughout the years. This slow process of change that occurs over millions of years is called **evolution**.

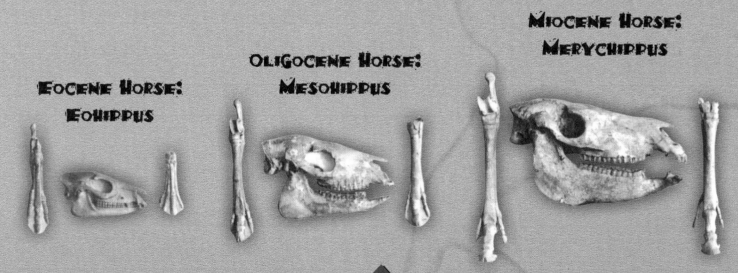

EOCENE HORSE: EOHIPPUS

OLIGOCENE HORSE: MESOHIPPUS

MIOCENE HORSE: MERYCHIPPUS

Fossils of some early horse species show how horses have evolved over time.

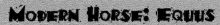

Modern Horse: Equus

Pleistocene Horse: Equus

Pliocene Horse: Hipparion

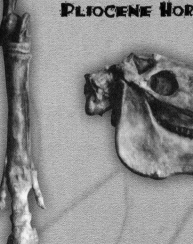

THE FIRST HORSE

Hyracotherium, the first horse, wasn't even as big as a medium-sized dog! This early horse species lived in the forests of North America, Asia, and Europe about 55 million years ago. This was after most of the non-flying dinosaurs had become **extinct**.

Hyracotherium looked like a mix between a deer and a horse. It had four toes on its front feet and three on its back feet. Its toes spread out when it walked. This helped Hyracotherium get around on the soft forest floor.

Hyracotherium and other early horses were **browsers**. This means they ate twigs and leaves from trees and bushes.

Hyracotherium, the first horse, lived on Earth about 55 million years ago.

THE HOOF AND A CHANGING HABITAT

As time passed, the **habitat**, or home, of the horse changed. When the climate got drier, some of the forests of North America turned into grasslands. This meant that the forest-dwelling horse had to **adapt** to its new home.

Two forms of the early horse developed as it **evolved** into the modern-day horse. These were **Mesohippus** and **Parahippus**. Instead of several toes on their feet, which had worked well on the forest floor, these early horses needed longer, stiffer legs and feet. This would help them run swiftly on the hard ground of the grasslands.

Over millions of years, the middle toe changed and became larger. The side toes slowly disappeared. The hoof of today's horse is really just one big toe!

When these early horses began to wander around on the grasslands, they also started to change what they ate. Some horses started to eat grass along with leaves and twigs.

Mesohippus roamed the dry grasslands of North America. This early horse had three toes. ▶

MERYCHIPPUS, THE FIRST GRAZER

Around 35 million years ago, horses in Asia and Europe had died out. So it was up to early horses in North America to evolve into today's horse.

Millions of years after Hyracotherium, the first type of horse, other ancient horses developed. One was called **Merychippus**, which lived about 20 million years ago. This horse looked a lot more like the modern-day horse. It was about four feet tall.

Merychippus looked similar to today's horse. This early horse was the first species to eat only grass.

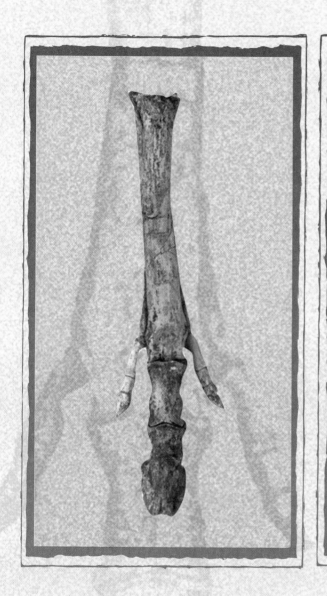

Merychippus was the first **grazer**. It was the first horse to eat only grass.

This grazer had one large middle toe and two small side toes. Only the middle toe was used to support the weight of the horse.

Herds of Merychippus once roamed the plains in what is today the state of Nebraska.

MIGRATION AND EXTINCTION

About two million years ago, horses as we know them appeared. Many of these horses **migrated** from North America to Asia and Europe. If you look at a world map, you'll see that these continents, or large areas of land, are separated by water. So how did horses travel from North America to Asia and Europe?

Millions of years ago, several land bridges linked North America and Asia. The horses traveled across these bridges.

Millions of years ago, horses traveled across land bridges that linked North America to Asia and Europe. ▶

Today, these land bridges are covered by the ocean. Over 10,000 years ago, the water from the melting ice of the last **Ice Age** covered the land bridges.

The horses that stayed in North America died out, possibly from the spread of disease. But the ones that traveled to Asia and Europe survived.

TAMING OF THE HORSE

Between 4,000 and 6,000 years ago, wild horses were first **tamed** by people in Asia and Europe. The Asian and European people kept herds of horses. They used horses to carry heavy items. They also ate the meat of the horses and used the skins to make clothes and shelter.

As horses became more tame, people began to ride them. Horses became a great way for people to get from place to place. Europeans brought the horse back with them around 500 years ago, when they invaded North America. Soon Native Americans began to raise and care for horses, and helped to spread them around the continent.

Native Americans, like the Sioux, helped to tame wild horses so that they could ride them.

HORSES TODAY

Many kinds of horses live in the world today. Since horses were tamed, humans have **bred** them for different uses.

Huge workhorses, such as **Clydesdales**, are raised to do heavy farmwork like pulling plows. Farmers choose the biggest and strongest Clydesdales to breed with each other. That way, they will have baby horses that will grow big and strong like their parents.

Clydesdales are very large horses that help farmers do their work. ▶

MORE MODERN-DAY HORSES

Have you ever heard the thundering hooves of **Thoroughbred** horses racing around a track? These slick, swift horses were bred from **Arabian** horses. Today's Thoroughbred horses are the distant relatives of three Arabian horses that lived over 300 years ago!

A few herds of wild horses, called **mustangs**, live in the western part of the United States. These animals come from horses that once belonged to Spanish **conquerors**, cowboys, and Native Americans.

Mustangs are very special. They remind us of the spirit and history of our country. Laws have been passed to protect mustangs, and to allow them to roam free from harm.

Wild horses, like these, roam free in Nevada and other western states in the United States.

▼

HORSES THROUGH THE YEARS

Some of the horse's characteristics have stayed the same over time. For example, prehistoric horses ate plants, much like today's horses do. Also, horses of the past lived in herds, and many modern-day horses travel in herds. But some things have changed. The horse adapted to where it lived in order to survive. The horse has grown and changed over millions of years, galloping through time into the tall, graceful animal we know today.

WEB SITE:

http://www.horsenet.com/pavilion/equivid/equivid.html

Glossary

adapt (uh-DAPT) To change to fit different conditions.

Arabian (uh-RAY-bee-un) A kind of horse that racing horses come from.

breed (BREED)   To produce young; to mate animals for the result of producing babies.

browser (BROW-zer) An animal that eats leaves and twigs from trees and shrubs.

Clydesdale (KLYDZ-dayl) A very large horse used for farmwork.

conquerer (KON-ker-er) A person who takes over an area, such as a country, and claims it for himself.

evolution (eh-vuh-LOO-shun) A slow process of change and development that living things go through over many, many years.

evolve (ee-VOLV) To develop or change over time.

extinct (ek-STINKT) When a certain kind of animal no longer exists.

fossil (FAH-sul) The hardened remains of a dead plant or animal.

grazer (GRAY-zer) An animal that eats grass and other plants from the ground.

habitat (HAB-ih-tat) The surroundings or area in which an animal lives.

Hyracotherium (hy-reh-ko-THEER-ee-um) The very first horse.

Ice Age (EYS AYJ) A long period of time thousands of years ago when most of the northern part of Earth was covered with glaciers, or large chunks of ice.

Merychippus (mehr-ee-KIP-us) An early horse of North America that was the first to feed on only grass.

Mesohippus (MES-oh-hip-us) An early horse that roamed the forests and grasslands of North America.

migrate (MY-grayt) When a large number of animals or people move to a different place to live.

mustang (MUS-tayng) One kind of wild horse that lives in the United States.

Parahippus (PAYR-uh-hip-us) An early horse that roamed the forests and grasslands of North America.

prehistoric (pree-his-TOR-ik) Happening before recorded history.

species (SPEE-sheez) A group of plants or animals that are very much alike.

tame (TAYM) To make calm, to change from being wild.

Thoroughbred (THOR-oh-bred)   A special kind of horse that is used for racing.

INDEX